Bufano

RANDOLPH FALK, 1939–

CELESTIAL ARTS
Millbrae, California c1975

Published by Celestial Arts
231 Adrian Road, Millbrae, California 94030

First Printing, August 1975
Made in the United States of America

Art direction and cover
design by Marek A. Majewski

Design by Dale Smith

Library of Congress Cataloging in Publication Data

Falk, Randolph, 1939-
Bufano.

Bibliography: P
1. Bufano, Beniamino, 1898-1970.
NB237, B76F34   730'.92'4   75-9069
ISBN 0-89087-175-2
ISBN 0-89087-061-6 pbk.

INTRODUCTION

I knew Beniamino Bufano only during the last three years of
his life.

In order to photograph him it was necessary for me to become
his chauffeur, business agent and almost constant companion.

He was often demanding and unpredictable. Without warning he
could be amiable one minute, tempestuous the next.

There were times when I was able to photograph unnoticed and
there were times when he told me to put aside my camera and help
with more important tasks! I always did.

Labeled everything from phony to genius, Bufano was always the
center of controversy. Called by some an egotist, clown, publicity
hound and troublemaker, to others he was a "pixie" or a "saint."

While some critics refer to his sculptures as trite, others consider
them major contributions to the world of art. But Benny didn't
create his works for art critics. His life was devoted to peace and
peace is the constant theme in his art.

*My sculptures are meant to speak of peace and the dignity
of man. If they in any way help bring an end to folly or place a
cobblestone in the road to peace, I shall have done my part.*

When I began photographing Bufano, he was very aware of my presence and the resulting photographs were rigid and unnatural. For too long he had, by choice and demand, struck familiar poses in front of the camera for the press and the souvenir collector. To Benny, photography was documentation and its worth was simply what it illustrated. A photograph of Bufano was a photograph of Bufano and nothing more. He was the substance.

The more I photographed, the more suspicious he became and on numerous occasions his patience wore thin. To protect myself from being ousted from his studio, I began assisting with his work. My assistance came to be expected and it wasn't long before I was totally immersed in Bufano. I became his "right-hand man," and I became his friend.

Our friendship tended to be one-sided (in his favor) and not without frustration, but it was exhilarating. I watched him maneuver his five-foot frame through life with great precision and skill, and I was genuinely impressed. And there was such a peaceful side to Bufano. He loved the country and often called on me to drive him there.

"Why me?" I asked one day on the way to Mt. Tamalpais. "Why is it whenever you want rest, you call on me?" Stifling a yawn he smiled, "Because you keep your mouth shut."

And so I did.

Such familiarity with Bufano provided the opportunity to observe him without being observed, and once that happened, once I could be invisible in his presence, I was able to photograph him as he was.

CONTENTS

BUFANO   I
HIS ART   85
PUBLIC ART   III

For
Joyce
and
Erica

A special thanks to Ansel Adams, Erskine Bufano, Leo Hills, Virginia Lewin, Aloha Nielsen, Ernest Rook, Joe Rosenthal, The Bufano Society of the Arts, and to the unidentified photographers whose photographs appear in the pages of this book for their contributions and assistance.

Bufano

Some sources suggest Bufano was born in 1889, most publications give 1898 as the year of his birth. Neither date was accepted by Benny.

Before autographing a recent book on his art, he scratched a line through 1898 and inserted 1910. His passports received the same alteration. Paradoxically, he claimed to have created statues for the Panama-Pacific Exposition held in San Francisco in 1915.

But whether Bufano died at age 81 or 72 or 103 doesn't really matter. What is impressive was his determination to live. One ingredient in his recipe for longevity was hard work. Even after a series of mild heart attacks he worked as though he were 17, trying to ignore signs of aging and ill health.

Benny's studio was filled with many tools, conventional and otherwise. There was a strange apparatus used for rounding out metal which consisted of a bowling ball with a handle protruding from a finger hole and set in a frame of logs and raw timber. The chisel and hammer so commonly associated with a sculptor of hard materials could be found, but were no longer being used. Metal files, used for smoothing the rough seams and edges of copper and stainless steel, were also there as a reminder of some of Benny's largest works. But their use was now limited to rounding off soft sculptures and the openings between the cutting edges were becoming filled with plaster dust. There were wood mallets for pounding out copper and a welder's mask, used for riveting, hung in one corner of the studio. Electric polishers were constantly being used to smooth stone sculptures already smoothed by careful molding. Benny's fingers must have been as sensitive as those of a blind person. He carefully caressed his sculptures seeking out the slightest imperfection and if one was found, the polisher started again. Then he painstakingly went over every piece by hand with emery cloth until they were as smooth as glass.

At times it was difficult to keep up with him. On one occasion when I was helping him move a large block of granite, he became aware of my panting. Without looking up he exclaimed, "You're young. What are you grunting for? You sound like a pig!"

But while his spirit was high and determination strong his youthful energy was waning. Long periods of hard work were interrupted by an almost embarrassing need to get out of the studio. His typical day involved numerous activities more and more directed away from physical involvement. It was sad to see Benny angry at himself for not being able to work straight through a long day, and reminders that he was doing twenty times that of someone his age were of no avail.

Bufano believed if he planned on living forever, he would. To keep dust out of his lungs when polishing his sculpture, he often wore a surgical mask. Although he used them sparingly, six months before his death, he insisted on buying a box of 1,000!

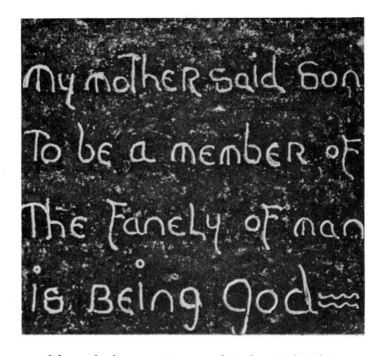

My mother said son
To be a member of
The family of man
is Being god

Although the exact year of Bufano's birth is obscure, it is known he was born in San Fele, Italy (near Rome) the youngest of sixteen children. Shortly after his third birthday, his family immigrated to New York. There he studied with several sculptors, including Paul Manship and John Fraser before coming to California in 1915. (While serving his apprenticeship with Fraser, he claimed to have made the mold for the buffalo on the buffalo nickel and to have been the model for the Indian on the reverse.)

Benny was, by choice, a man of few words. "Talk is cheap. It's action that counts," he often said. "I'm not interested in what a person says but what he does." In many ways this attitude was a convenience for him. It prevented him from having to answer what he considered "foolish questions," and from having to reveal himself or justify his art. Too many questions made him nervous. His quiet manner added greatly to his mysteriousness. People who knew him for twenty or thirty years are often at a loss to describe him.

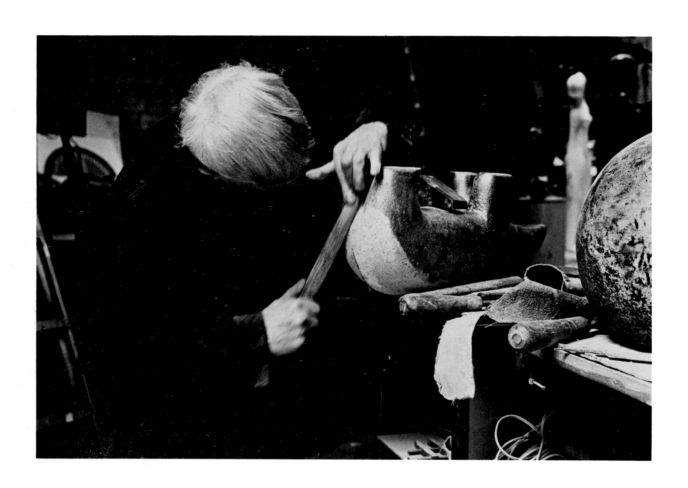

People interferred with his work and he ignored them as much as he could. His family was no exception. He denied ever having been married or the existence of his two children.

One morning while he finished some work in his studio, he told me someone would be arriving soon, and asked if I would join them for lunch. Within minutes, an attractive woman arrived and the three of us walked a few yards to a cafe adjoining his studio. Benny made no introduction, and conversation was awkward. Only after he left the table (to complain to the waitress for buttering his toast) did I learn the woman was his daughter. He never revealed her identity to me.

That my forms lack detail
by no means indicates
a lack of knowledge of anatomy.
In fact, I learned it so well as a child,
it took me twenty years to forget it.

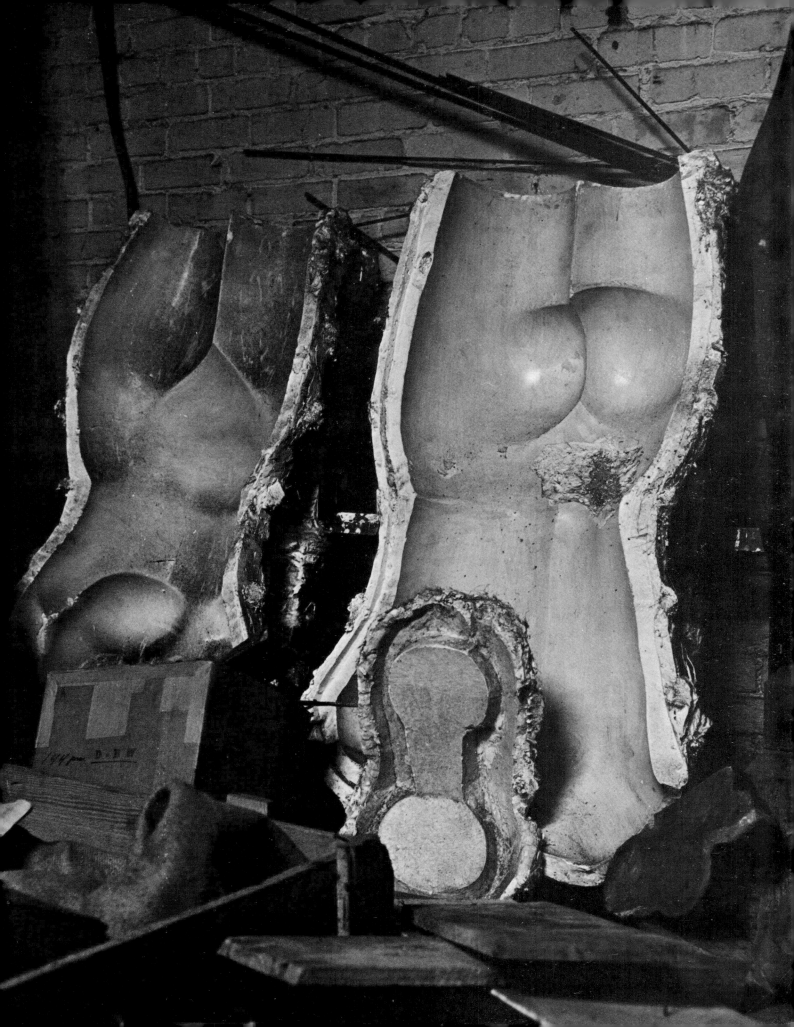

Although widely recognized, Bufano had few friends. He didn't associate with other artists and rarely acknowledged their existence. The most generous statement I heard him make about another artist's work was, "It's O.K."

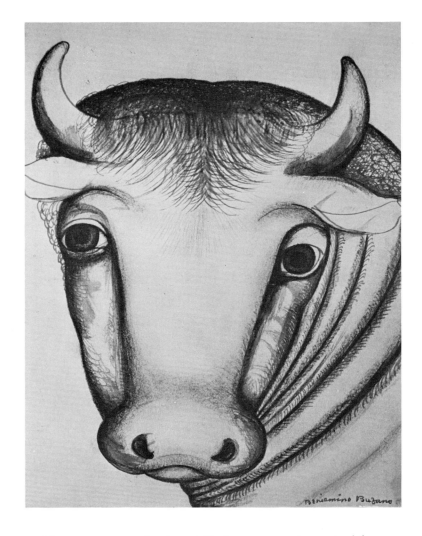

However, much about Bufano compensated for, or at least made tolerable, his disrespect and selfishness. In the privacy of his studio or the countryside, he revealed a sensitive and loving personality. Although conversation was simple and usually brief, it was always emotional. He talked about children, nature, and politics. On the latter subject he was always critical, because what he talked about was the ending of war and the creation of permanent peace. He saw little being done about either and was frustrated by the futility of his own efforts toward those goals.

Much of the time Benny reminisced or simply let his mind wander, and he loved to tell stories—especially Bufano stories! Some he told so many times it was difficult to respond any longer. Through them he gave the impression that whatever greatness or accomplishment he had achieved was in the past. He seemed restless with the present, but spoke of future plans as though life had no ending.

Sculptures were Bufano's "money" and he bartered with the doctor, the dentist and the lawyer. Beyond these essential services, his needs were extremely simple. They consisted of a place to work, a place to sleep, and just enough food to keep him alive — none of which cost him a cent. His studio rent was paid by a friend, his room at the Press Club was free, and he ate at several restaurants "on the house." Nevertheless, he despised waste.

Once, while driving past an orchard, he saw hundreds of apples rotting on the ground. He asked me to stop, jumped out of the car, and gathered as many apples as he could. Along with bread, which he dried to preserve, this was his lunch for the next several weeks.

His dress was usually shabby. On many occasions, I saw him brush the dust off his work clothes with a shoe brush, file his fingernails with a metal file from his workbench, then set off for an appointment. And he only went to that much trouble if he was meeting someone important!

He did have a few suits made in exchange for some sculptures, but on the rare occasions he wore one, his appearance was not significantly improved — especially if, in an attempt to look a few years younger, he applied shoe polish to his hair.

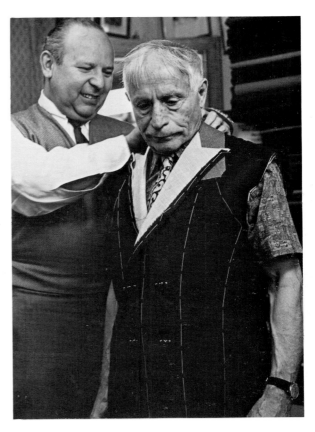

While he wasn't at all concerned about his dress, that same attitude did not apply to the materials used in his work. Marble had to be the finest, and was often obtained from the quarries in Italy near the village where he was born. Mosaic tiles had to be exceptionally vibrant in color and unusually durable. The metal for his sculptures had to be nothing less than stainless steel.

It was extremely rare for Bufano to sign or date his works — a phenomenon which caused much speculation. When asked about this, Benny usually replied with one of two answers: "Everything I create belongs to the people" or "Christ, how can anyone mistake a Bufano?"

Considering how long it took to create most of his works, Bufano was extraordinarily prolific. Even though he gave away several pieces, and many others were destroyed by fire or vandalism, he left several hundred completed works in his estate.

As his life, he wanted his creations to last forever. And he wanted them to be seen. He said that people kept stealing his smaller sculptures so he decided to make them so large that, "no one could possibly carry them away."

But this created different problems. Sheer unmanageable size, or lack of money or equipment for proper installation, often meant a piece was neglected for a time or forgotten entirely. His monument to peace located at Timber Cove Inn was no exception. Five years after completion, it remained unassembled on a bluff overlooking the Pacific Ocean, 90 miles north of San Francisco. The problem was how to raise the huge head and hand atop the 70-foot body.

During the fall of 1969, at the request of the Bufano Society of the Arts, a rigging company managed to get a truck and long boom up the narrow, winding coast highway to do the job. Benny was at his studio in Italy, but a number of fans and curious spectators were there to see the statue completed. Benny and I had often visited the site and he had talked excitedly about completing the statue. He told me his statue symbolized the unity of all nations and was to look out over the ocean as a friendly gesture of peace. However, when the head was lowered into position over a previously welded framework, it didn't fit — not if it was to face the ocean. A decision was made to change the framework and the head and hand were placed into position.

When Bufano returned from Italy a few weeks later, I anxiously told him about the "surprise." The next day we drove up the coast to see his dream completed. Along the way, I mentioned the difficulty we had had in fitting the head over the framework, and told Benny of the necessary changes. But by then, I was beginning to have doubts about changing the framework. What Benny said made me realize it shouldn't have been. "If that head is on backwards, I'm going to blow the son-of-a-bitch up! How could you put it on backwards? It would only fit one way!" It was a convincing argument. The remainder of the drive was spent in absolute silence.

When we arrived at the statue Benny looked up and, not being able to see the top (his eyesight was failing), asked me to show him which direction the head was facing. I managed to point a shaky arm toward the ocean while reminding him that this was the direction we had discussed. Swinging his arm wildly over his head, he yelled, "You idiot! Look around! The water is everywhere! Only the seals can see the face the way it is now!"

Then he took me to the base of the statue and parted some weeds. "Look at the feet! How can the toes point one direction and the face another?" It was another convincing argument.

After an hour or so, Benny calmed down enough to discuss a possible solution. He finally decided he would add another face of mosaic tiles to the back of the existing head.

Today the statue stands looking two directions — across the ocean as a symbol of peace and, as Benny put it, "toward the highway so people can see the damn thing!"

Benny walked from his small room at the San Francisco Press Club to his studio on Minna Street every morning. Along the way he was greeted by dozens of admirers before stopping to have a breakfast of yogurt and fruit at a cafeteria which housed three of his largest mosaics (now located at the Holiday Inn in Los Banos, California). The remainder of the walk was a short one, and he arrived at his studio before most people arrived at their jobs. Sometimes he attempted to tidy up, made phone calls, or read the morning paper before launching into his work. Most of the time, however, he began working on whatever he reluctantly left unfinished the night before.

Occasionally he had visitors. They were often school children whose teacher had arranged for a tour of his studio. Benny loved them and eagerly demonstrated his skills whenever he could coax them down from his sculptures.

"Look how much children appreciate my animals," he would say, "why can't adults be more like that?"

One morning he invited a beautiful Vietnamese girl to his
studio. The victim of a napalm attack, she was in San
Francisco for corrective surgery. She was awed by Benny and
his sculptures and they rapidly became friends. When she
left the studio, Benny's eyes filled with tears, he was so
enraged by her disfiguration. During the time she was in San
Francisco, he wrote a paper criticizing our involvement in
the Vietnam War entitled, "WE ARE ALL MURDERERS."

During the fifties it was not uncommon for conservatives to label Bufano a communist because of his liberal political views.

While he was in disfavor there were complaints that Saint Francis, which stood in the center of the main stairway of the Church of Saint Francis, was in the way of wedding and funeral processions.

When Bufano was told his renowned statue would have to be moved he was overcome with indignation. Then, in typical behavior, he pointed out that Saint Francis was only the *central figure* in a planned grouping of three and began elaborating on his plans to install the others.

Shortly thereafter Saint Francis was on its way to Oakland.

Because of the convenience of nearby quarries, Benny's marble sculptures were carved at his studio in Italy. He went there at least once a year to work, and when enough pieces were completed to warrant a shipment home, he eagerly awaited their arrival. When they did arrive, he uncrated them with all the excitement of a child opening a Christmas present. It was always a joy to be around him until the last crate was unpacked. Then came the problem of what to do with them. Because of their size, it was always difficult to find suitable storage space. Benny never worried about such practical matters until they were upon him. Even then, he worried very little. Fortunately, there were people who were concerned, and somehow his sculptures found their way to a suitable location — at least temporarily.

So he could devote maximum time to his creations, Benny organized a group of people to manage his business affairs. First established in 1946 as Bufano Studios, Inc., the group later became The Bufano Society of the Arts. Composed of prominent and influential citizens, the group was very effective in handling matters which Benny would otherwise ignore or probably botch. However, efficiency was not always compatible with Benny's interests and meetings rarely went smoothly. In the end, whatever Bufano wanted, Bufano got.

Although only five feet tall, Benny dreamed of enormous creations and made models for several. Two of his aspirations were to cover Yosemite's El Capitan with a mosaic Saint Francis and to erect an 800-foot steel arch on Alcatraz Island. Yet, he created hundreds of shy, gentle animals of more realistic proportions.

I am not interested in what we cannot do, only what we can do interests me ... I know nothing in man's makeup that is not possible and complete.

When Benny wanted something, he felt the quickest way to obtain it was to go directly to the source. He rarely phoned ahead and often found himself waiting to see someone, or worse, found no one in at all.

Upset over a legal difficulty, he walked a mile and a half from his studio to his attorney's office. After learning of his whereabouts, he walked another three blocks to City Hall and into a courtroom, where he waited until court recessed to air his problem.

For a time during the forties, Benny lived in Big Sur, the rugged redwood country south of San Francisco. Having no money for materials, he carved statues out of indigenous redwood and oak. The most significant was a set of five figures representing the crucifixion, which he called, "Man's Inhumanity to Man." In addition, he carved yet another Saint Francis, a huge redwood owl, an enormous redwood hand, and fashioned a harp out of a large limb which he fitted with piano strings. With a few exceptions, these are the only "soft" sculptures Benny ever made.

*I'm not a religious man in the orthodox
sense. Why Hell, there's as much corruption
in the Vatican as there is in our society...
the whole world is my temple and I treat
everything with great respect... I even try not
to walk too hard on the floor
boards of my studio.*

Although Benny claimed he was "not a religious man in the orthodox sense," there are significant indications to the contrary. His creation of a bronze relief dramatically illustrates his identification with Christ. He made a life-size crucifixion with the index finger of the right hand missing — the same finger Benny cut off his own hand, either intentionally or accidentally, years before! In its place protrudes a single flower, a symbol of peace.

In Benny's studio, on the very day of his death, I found a new sketch for a mosaic of himself with Pope John. A tear suspends delicately beneath the Pope's eye.

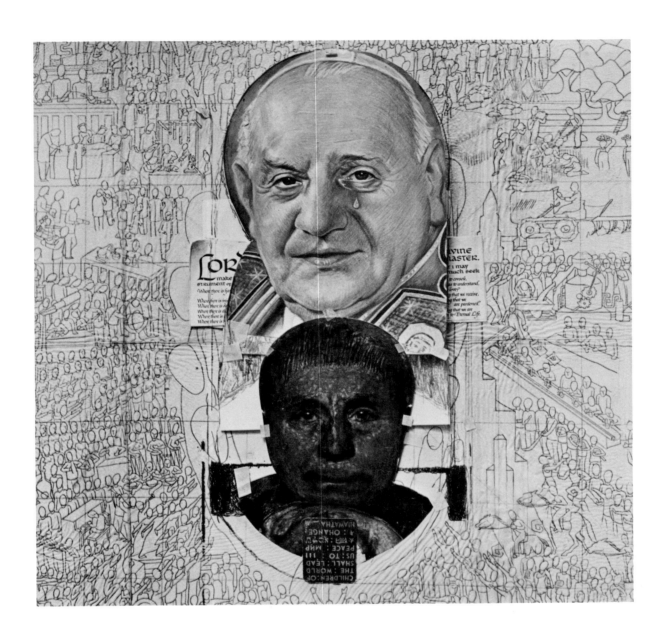

As I stepped from the car, on the day of Benny's funeral, I was handed this note by a boy of about thirteen:

The little man in the big City, the City
that was his own.
And so the City turns out for his death;
just to be on television, they liked his work
or they liked him.

All I know is he sculpted the bear in
Sunnydale; that beautiful black bear.
His art points to Heaven.

You must be very courageous to ride here and
let the City gawk at you.
Do not be depressed by us.
We know of him in only little ways, and many
are here because they are honestly sorrowful.

Peace of Christ be with you!

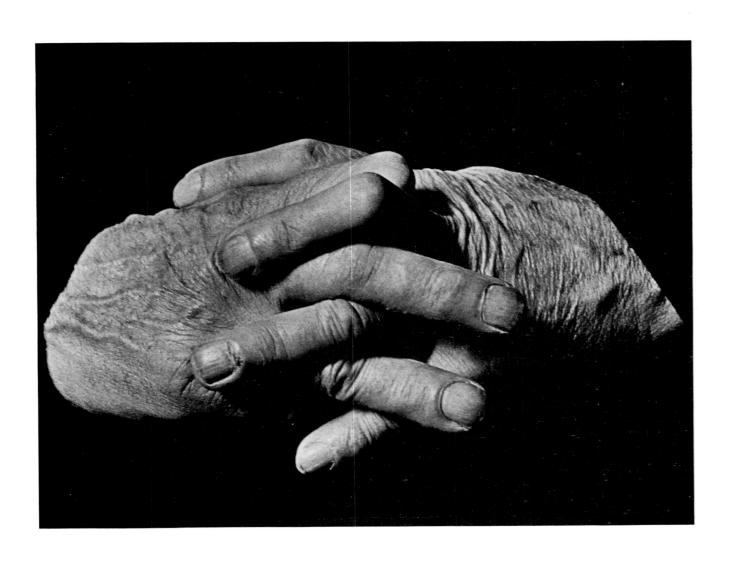

Ansel Adams

CRUCIFIXION
Cast bronze **1924** Bufano Society of the Arts

84

HIS ART

THE SAN FRANCISCO PRESS CLUB CAT
Mosaic   1950s   Bufano Society of the Arts

MIRACLE OF THE LOAVES AND FISH
Mosaic   1940s   Bufano Society of the Arts

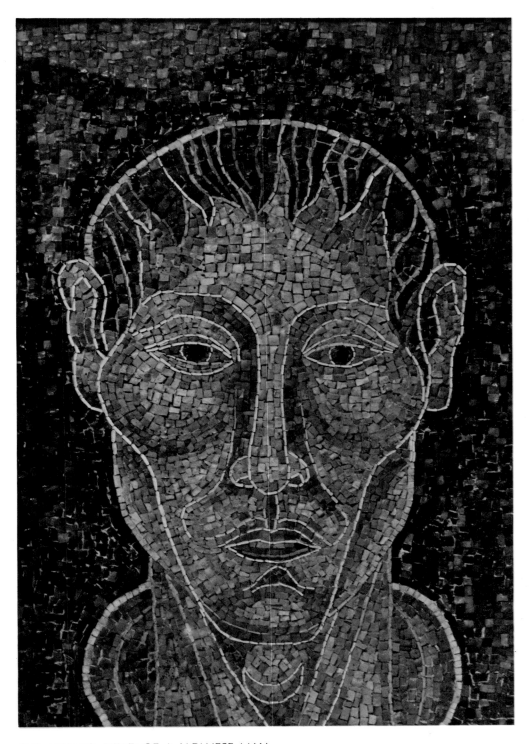

THE ASCETIC: HEAD OF A JAPANESE MAN
Mosaic   1930s   Bufano Society of the Arts

UNIVERSAL FACE for base of peace statue
Mosaic inset at base of a 60-foot, 12-ton cast granite aggregate statue; completed in June 1970, it was Bufano's last major work depicting peace. The face is in three colors: white, yellow and black (actually dark gray and purple) representing the three races. Bufano frequently used the "universal" face in his mosaics.
Bufano Society of the Arts

SNAIL
White Carrara marble   1960's   Bufano Society of the Arts

HEDGEHOG
Cast bronze   1960s

PENGUIN
Cast bronze   1960s

POLAR BEAR
Cast silver   1950s

OWL
Cast silver   1950s

CAT
Ceramic   1960s

(Miniature)   Bufano Society of the Arts

OWL and RABBIT (Miniatures)
Cast bronze   1960s   Bufano Society of the Arts

RABBIT
White Carrara marble   1960s   Bufano Society of the Arts

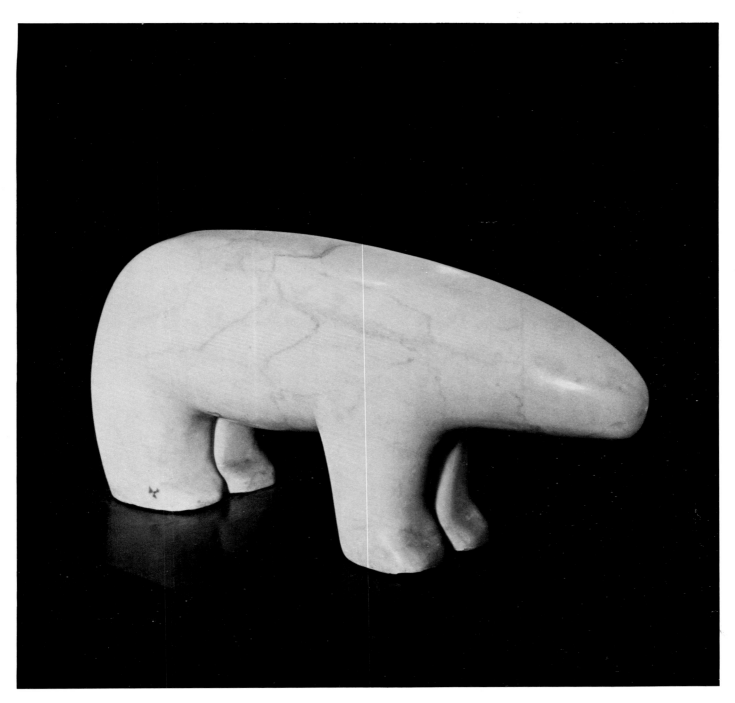

POLAR BEAR
White marble   1950s   Bufano Society of the Arts

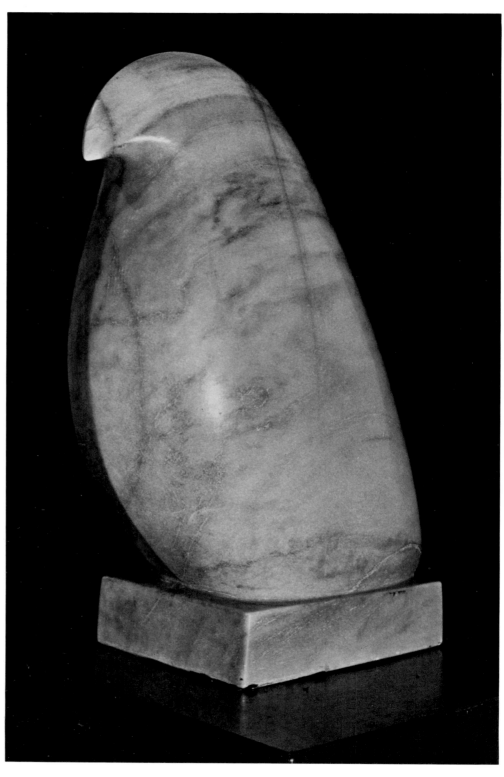

PARROT
Pink marble   1960s   Bufano Society of the Arts

RAM
Orange Portuguese marble   1940s   Bufano Society of the Arts

RAM (Miniature)
Solid cast bronze   1950s   Private collection

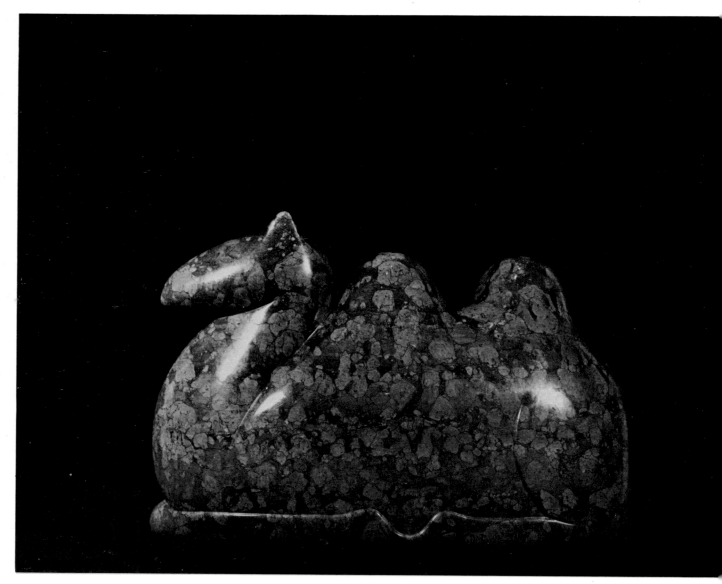

BACTRIAN CAMEL
96   Orange Portuguese marble   1950s   Bufano Society of the Arts

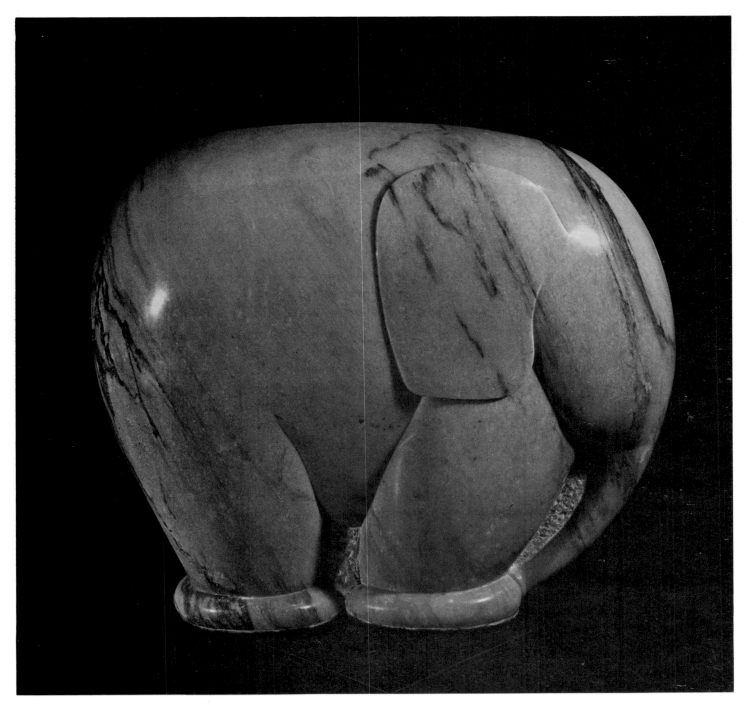

ELEPHANT
Pink marble   1960s   Bufano Society of the Arts

DUCK
Light orange marble   1960s   Bufano Society of the Arts

ST. FRANCIS ON HORSEBACK
Yellow marble   1920s   Bufano Society of the Arts

BULL
Crayon and pencil drawing   1930s   Bufano Society of the Arts

BULL
Wax and crayon drawing   1930s   Bufano Society of the Arts

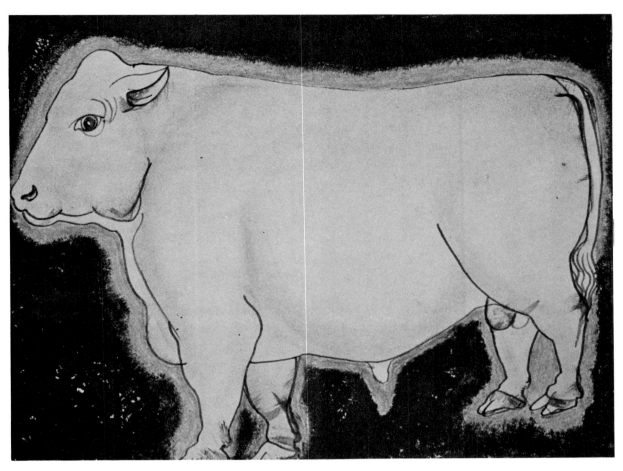

BULL
Wax and crayon drawing   1920s   Bufano Society of the Arts

PORTRAIT OF THE ARTIST AS CHILD
Wax and crayon drawing   1920s   Bufano Society of the Arts

PORTRAIT
Wax and crayon drawing   1920s   Bufano Society of the Arts

ST. FRANCIS
Pencil drawing   1920s   Bufano Society of the Arts

ST. FRANCIS
Lithograph   No date   Bufano Society of the Arts

CHINESE GIRL HOLDING FLOWER
Blue and red glazed terra cotta   1920s (China)   Private collection

CHINESE GIRL WITH BOWL OF RICE
Green glazed terra cotta   1920s (China)   Private collection

YOUNG GIRL
Red and blue glazed terra cotta   1920s   Private collection

CHINESE PHILOSOPHER
Green glazed terra cotta   1920s (China)   Private collection

ST. FRANCIS
Redwood   1940s   Bufano Society of the Arts
A beautiful example of Bufano's wood sculpture; considered
to be one of his finest works.

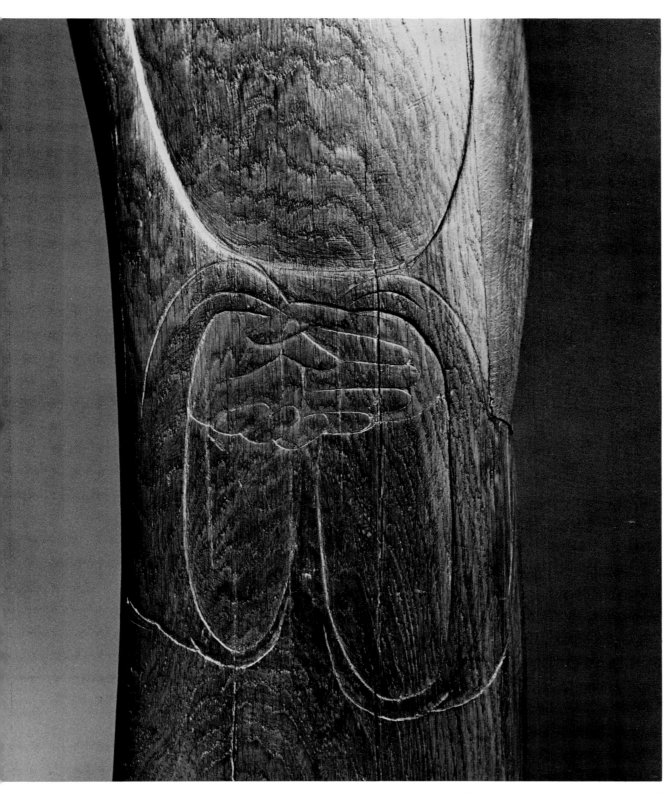

ST. FRANCIS (reverse)

SISTER OF THE ARTIST
Unglazed terra cotta   1920s (China)   Private collection

THE PUBLIC ART

NUDE TORSO
Granite   1930s
Extended loan from the M. H. de Young Musem. Located at California State
University, San Francisco, 19th and Holloway Avenue, in the quadrangle.

HEAD OF ST. FRANCIS
Polished granite on granite base   1938
W.P.A. (Works Progress Administration)
Located at California State University, San Francisco, 19th and Holloway
Avenues, in courtyard between Business and Humanities Buildings.

MOTHER OF THE ARTIST
Green, orange and black glazed terra cotta   1916
Loan from Stanford University Museum, Leon Liebes Bequest. Located at
Oakland Museum, 1000 Oak Street, Oakland.

LOUIS PASTEUR
Stainless steel and red granite   1940s   W.P. A.
Located at San Rafael High School,
185 Mission Street, San Rafael.

RABBIT
White cast granite   1930s
Located at Hillsdale Shopping Center, 60 Hillsdale Mall, San Mateo. Original,
black marble, located in housing project, Valencia Gardens, at 15th Street
between Valencia and Guerrero Streets, San Francisco.

CAT
Cast granite   1930s
Located at Hillsdale Shopping Center, 60 Hillsdale Mall, San Mateo; original,
marble, located at public housing project, Valencia Gardens, at 15th Street
between Valencia and Guerrero Streets, San Francisco.

BEAR AND NURSING CUBS
Cast granite   1930s
Oakland Museum, gift of Fenner Fuller family.
Located at the Oakland Museum, 1000 Oak Street, Oakland; original, red
porphyry, located in public housing project, Valencia Gardens, at 15th Street
between Valencia **and** Guerrero Streets, San Francisco. Considered by many
to be the best example of Bufano's numerous animals.
Other granite castings are located at:
California Academy of Sciences, Golden Gate Park, San Francisco; University of
California Medical Center, Millberry Union, 3rd and Parnassus Streets, San
Francisco; Marin County Humane Society, 171 Bel Marin Key Boulevard,
Novato; Hillsdale Shopping Center, 60 Hillsdale Mall, San Mateo.

ST. FRANCIS
Cast granite   1967, erected 1968   College of Notre Dame
Located at the College of Notre Dame, Belmont.

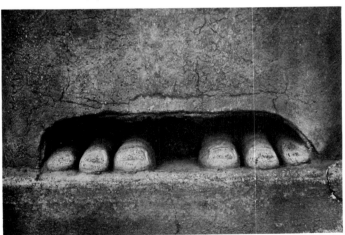

CAT AND MOUSE
Cast granite   1930s
Located at Hillsdale Shopping Center, 60 Hillsdale Mall, San Mateo; original,
marble, located at public housing project, Valencia Gardens, at 15th Street
between Valencia and Guerrero Streets, San Francisco.

CALIFORNIA BEAR over Head of Peace
Black granite   1930s   W.P.A.
Located at Hillsdale Shopping Center, 60 Hillsdale Mall, San Mateo; also,
Administration Building, Sunnydale Housing Project, 1654 Sunnydale Avenue,
San Francisco.

HAND OF PEACE
Copper, mosaic and stained glass   1967   Pacific Bridge Company
Located at 35 Quail Court, take stairway into upper courtyard, Walnut Creek.

PENGUINS
Red porphyry and stainless steel   1930s (restored 1960s)
Located at Golden Gateway Center, Davis Court, Jackson and Washington
Streets, San Francisco.

BEAR
Cast granite   No date
Gift to Town of Ross, presented by Mr. and Mrs. Jerome Flax in 1971.
Located at Ross Town Hall, Sir Francis Drake Boulevard, Ross.

MOUSE
Cast granite   1930s   W.P.A.
Located at Hillsdale Shopping Center; original, black granite, located at public
housing project, Valencia Gardens, at 15th Street between Valencia and
Guerrero Streets, San Francisco.

SEAL
Granite   1930s
Located at San Francisco Maritime Museum on the rear deck, foot of Polk
Street, San Francisco; also, Hillsdale Shopping Center, 60 Hillsdale Mall, San
Mateo.

OWL
Brown marble   1960s
The Cannery, Beach Street between Leavenworth and Hyde Streets, San
Francisco (in the main courtyard). Also at the Cannery:
ELEPHANT, brown marble, 1960s; FIGURE IN SPACE, mosaic and lead, 1950s;
LISTENING POSTS (2), mosaic, 1950s.

SHADOWS OF THE FUTURE
Black Belgian granite   1919   Leon Liebes bequest
Located in the courtyard behind the Student Union Building, Stanford
University, Palo Alto; also, courtyard of the Santa Rosa Public Library, Santa
Rosa. SHADOWS OF THE FUTURE is a simplified version of an original work in
terra cotta titled THE HONEYMOON COUPLE; it is a portrait of a young Chinese
couple Bufano knew during his stay in China.

ST. FRANCIS ON HORSEBACK
Cast black granite   1930s   W.P.A. Located at Hillsdale Shopping Center, San Mateo ;
also, Westside Courts between Scott and Baker Streets, Post and Sutter Streets,
San Francisco.

131

DOLLAROCRACY
Mosaic mural   1965   Warehousemen's Union
Located in the Longshoremen's Union, Local 6,
99 Hegenberger Road, Oakland; two other mosaic
murals, HUMANITY AT WORK and A LITTLE
CHILD SHALL LEAD THEM, are also at
the union hall.

FROG
Black granite   1930 s
Located at the San Francisco Maritime Museum
(rear deck), foot of Polk Street, Aquatic Park,
San Francisco. Also, in cast granite at the
Hillsdale Shopping Center, San Mateo.

SUN YAT-SEN
Stainless steel and rose-red granite   W.P.A.
Located in St. Mary's Plaza, San Francisco.
Steel disc inset at base is inscribed, "Father of the Chinese Republic and First
President (1921-1922)...Champion of Democracy...Proponent of Peace and
Friendship among Nations," words written by Lin Sen, President of China, 1937.

ST. FRANCIS
Cast granite   1939
Located at International Longshoreman's and Warehouseman's Union Hall,
Fisherman's Wharf, corner of Taylor and Beach Streets, San Francisco. Originally
placed at the Church of St. Francis in North Beach, San Francisco in 1955, it was
moved six years later after much controversy (see Page 61); following a brief
stay in Oakland, it was erected in its present location in 1962.